Advance Praise of *Earthling Love*

"It is such a pleasure and an honor to dip into, and linger a while, savoring Rob's life poetry of joy and elegance, sorrow and commitment. I feel enriched by the privilege of accompanying a wonderful human being through his life story and those things that needed the outreach/ voice of poetry to convey some touch of their essence."

— Peggy Rubin, founding director of the Center for Sacred Theatre in Ashland, Oregon; and principal teaching associate of Jean Houston, PhD

"The next frontier of the human race is in the heart. As exemplified by the poetry of Robertson Work, art leads us directly there. Through his poems, Robertson reveals a gentle yet awe-inspiring heartscape. Whether it is sorrow, anger, or joy, what is in Robertson's heart as expressed in his poem, is universal truth. When we listen for, express, and honor that truth, the world shifts. I am grateful for such an immense gift from Robertson."

— Qinghong Wei, PhD, artist, educator, and student of life

"Joy! Joy! Joy! for Roberson Work's poems. It has been said that human societies would be better off listening to poets than politicians. This is certainly demonstrated in this earthy, beautiful and powerful collection. His warm affection for life flows through the song of his verse. His earthly vows touch the heavenly realms of life's preciousness. A rainbow of tenderness shines in family beauty. This is a book written by a beloved friend of mine for many years. I suggest keeping it by one's bedside as I intend."

— Larry Ward, PhD, co-founder of The Lotus Institute;
Zen teacher in the Order of Interbeing

"These beautiful, poignant poems evoked so many emotions in me, from profound sadness to abundant joy. Robertson's *heartsong* is his innate ability to take us along on an intimate journey, which guides us to the realization that hope for a better tomorrow only depends upon our capacity to love and cherish all that is good within ourselves and the mosaic of humanity."

— Laura J. Bauer, MPA, executive director of the
Mattie J.T. Stepanek Foundation; teacher,
peacemaker, lover of all life

"I savored the poems slowly, like vintage Bordeaux. I have only beautiful things to say about the book because it evokes beauty, depth, soulfulness, faith, fidelity, and above all, love. The German word for fidelity or faithfulness is *die Treue*, akin to the English word "true". Richard Wagner's heroes such as Parsifal have this as a great virtue. I see the Rob of *Earthling Love* as a warrior-monk, either a Templar knight of Christ or a zen-practicing Ronin of Buddha, fighting for what is right but with compassion and love and without the senseless violence that many of his poems deplore. I see *Treue* in *Earthling Love - Treue* and steadfastness (*die Beharrlichkeit*) to many things, to people, to humanity, and to those he loves.

"*Earthling Love* is Robertson Work's melodious and rhythmic biography in verse. It must be read in conjunction with his insightful and touching autobiography, *Serving People & Planet: In Mystery, Love, and Gratitude* (SPP), because the poems mirror the many landmarks of the spiritual and temporal life of one who serves humanity. The poems are meant to be read aloud and serve as the soundtrack to SPP. In our cerebral, abstract, fragmented, and alienated modern world, *Earthling Love* reconnects us with our heart and spirit, delivering us from abstraction and egocentrism, and placing us firmly on the ground to join hands with the author in a shared ballet of earth, humanity, family, and self. His poems remind us that that we are not separate from those around us and from the world and souls who cradle and nourish us. The plea of *Earthling Love* is for us to nourish all of them in return with lovingkindness, compassion, and joy."

— Nikhil Chandavarkar, PhD, founder and CEO of Thersus Sustainability, and author of historical fiction; former UN senior official for thirty-six years

EARTHLING LOVE

Also by Robertson Work

Book author
Serving People & Planet: In Mystery, Love and Gratitude

*A Compassionate Civilization: The Urgency of Sustainable
Development and Mindful Activism – Reflections and
Recommendations*

Chapter author
Changing Lives, Changing Societies
Decentralization and Power-Shift
Engaging Civil Society
*Life Lessons for Loving the Way You Live
(Chicken Soup for the Soul)*
New Regional Development Paradigms: Vol. 3
Reinventing Government for the 21st Century

General editor and contributor
Participatory Local Governance
Pro-Poor Urban Governance: Lessons from LIFE 1992-2005

Contributor
Cities, People and Poverty: UNDP Urban Strategy
Re-conceptualizing Governance
The Urban Environment

EARTHLING LOVE

Living poems

1965 – 2020

Robertson Work

ISBN: 978-0-578-71125-6

Library of Congress Control Number: 2020911368

Because of the dynamic nature of the Internet, any web addresses or links contained in this book may have changed since publication and may no longer be valid. The views expressed in this work are solely those of the author and do not necessarily reflect the views of the publisher, and the publisher hereby disclaims any responsibility for them.

Compassionate Civilization Press
Swannanoa, North Carolina
28778 USA

DEDICATION

This book of poems is dedicated to
Bonnie Myotai Treace, profound poet,
author, and Zen teacher - my beloved wife,
and GrandBonnie

CONTENTS

PREFACE

Why have I written poetry on and off during my adult life when my professional service and writing have focused on enabling sustainable and just development and leadership in communities, organizations, individuals, and countries? The practice of writing poems has been for me a personal commitment to truth telling, of interrupting the rational, analytical mind, and of painting a vast vision that includes galaxies *and* flowers. I have been driven to poetry to express deep emotions, to honor loved ones, and to express radical aliveness in a fleeting moment. And, I have been called by the poetic arts as a way to share my personal observations, reflections, stories, and decisions.

Now in 2020, I had the impulse to make these modest poems public. I am aware, as are many, that the world is beset with the pain of climate chaos, ecocide, a viral pandemic, racism, wealth inequality, and much more. In some sense, I am sharing these poems now because they are part of how I stay sane and happy and in touch with what is beautiful, energizing, and meaningful, as I try to create a better world. May they touch your mind and heart as well.

The poems are arranged in two collections: poems celebrating Earth and humanity; and poems commemorating family and self. The poems celebrating Earth remind us of the vast universe, galaxy, and solar system of which we are part. They celebrate the precious gift of being a member of the Earth community. They call us to care for the Earth as loyal Earthlings. They paint a vision of an exquisite mountain, a mighty river, a blue sky, ducks, and trees. The poems celebrating humanity remind us that there is one human race with a rich diversity of wisdom, behaviors, cultures, and social systems. The poems commemorating family honor a grandparent, wife, children, and grandchildren. They grieve the death of a spouse with sorrow and honesty. They urge onward the young. They express excitement and gratitude for new love. And, the poems commemorating being one small Earthling share some wisdom of letting go, paying attention, kindness, and vowing to be happy.

I wrote the eighty-two poems in this book during fifty-five years, from twenty to seventy-five years of age, 1965 to 2020. Major themes include: wisdom, the ultimate, love of family, death and grief, falling in love, the beauty of the Hudson River, and contemplation of planet Earth. Other themes include: war and peace, mystery, dialogue, life, love, pilgrimages, the cosmos, dance, and social artistry. They were written to be read aloud. I love the sound of the words, the alliterations, the word plays, the repetitions, the surprises, the drama of it all.

The earliest is an anti-war poem written in 1965 when I was a student and activist at Oklahoma State University and published in OSU's "Soliloquy." Four other poems were also published at that time, the first in 1963 when I was eighteen. The next poem I wrote was almost a decade later in 1974 commemorating the adoption of my son in Seoul, Republic of Korea. Then, after another ten years, in 1984, seven family poems were written in Kingston, Jamaica. In Caracas, Venezuela, I wrote twelve in 1987 - 1990. This was a dynamic time of the dissolution of the family association of the nonprofit we were part of, the Institute of Cultural Affairs (ICA), the exploration of new ways of thinking and meditating, and encountering the creative work of Jean Houston, PhD, in releasing human potential. Then, while with the UN, in 1990, I wrote one poem in New York City, and one in Peekskill, NY, in 1993. My most prolific period was in Garrison, NY, where I wrote forty-five poems – over half of the book – from 2000 to 2006; this included the period after which my wife passed away and when I fell in love again. In 2007, I wrote two poems in Delphi, Greece, and Haliburton, Canada, and in 2014, seven poems in Cold Spring, NY, after launching the *Compassionate Civilization* blog. Finally, in Swannanoa, NC, living near the grandchildren, I wrote five poems in 2018 – 2020.

With academic training in English literature, linguistics and theology, I have always loved words, language, poetry, and nonfiction. Some of my favorite American and English poets include Emily Dickinson, Walt Whitman, e. e. cummings, T. S. Eliot, Carl Sandburg, Robert Frost, and D. H. Lawrence; and favorite non-English poets include Nikos Kazantzakis, Rumi, and Rilke. In addition to this book of poems, I have published two previous books, a memoir/autobiography, *Serving People & Planet: In Mystery, Love and Gratitude*, and a manifesto/handbook, *A Compassionate Civilization*. As part of my work in the UN, I also wrote chapters in six books, and was general-editor or contributor for five others. I have written numerous speeches, policy papers, course syllabi, essays, journal entries, blog posts, and social media posts. Words, of course, are not merely auditory or visual signs. They combust in the brain, between people, and in society-at-large, creating and changing the human and natural world. In the case of poetry, an individual poem is a personal gesture of truth telling and loving in this glorious, suffering world.

The great poets mentioned above changed my world with their poems. I could suddenly see and feel things I had not seen or felt before. I could hear provocative music. I tasted strange, new delights. I gained new language and understanding about the gift of being alive, new truths to guide me, new ways to express my love as an Earthling in living poems.

May the poems in this book be of service to you

APOLOGIA POETICA

Mere words strung
vertically upon a page
or two
rather old fashion
communicating
feeling and thought of
one person
some would say elitist
certainly not mass media
no flowing sights of color
as in video movie TV
no satellites spinning round
beaming electrons
to white dishes and antennae
earth bound
but markings on paper
pre-requisite literacy
signaling meaning
transferred from one mind
to another
an intimate dialogue

COLLECTION ONE

Poems Celebrating Earth and Humanity

STARLIGHT BURNS

Starlight burns
And brightens the
Morning air
Earth is such a
Splendid place
To live!

EARTHRISE ALIVE

Now you see it (my dear God!)
for the first time (since the beginning)
suspended in the void
Black Space
There (yet Here)
a swirl of blues greens whites
a ball
so round round round (like a painted melon)
The Earth
our planet
our place
in the Cosmos -
Space — vast beyond imagining
(empty) yet Full
of violent energy
starry explosions
surrounded by silence, stillness
the Creation in process
Now you see it
but not forever
for now you be it
Be it

THE WONDER OF BEING A SPECK

Compared to the Universe, the Milky Way is just a speck
Compared to the Milky Way, our Solar System is just a
    speck
Compared to the Solar System, our planet Earth is just
    a speck
Compared to the Earth, the New York metropolitan
    area is just a speck
Compared to the New York metropolitan area, Garrison
    is just a speck
Compared to Garrison, my house is just a speck
Compared to my house, I am just a speck
Compared to me, my little toe is just a speck
Compared to my little toe, a toe cell is just a speck
Compared to a toe cell, a toe molecule is just a speck
Compared to a toe molecule, an atom is just a speck
Compared to an atom, an electron is just a speck
Compared to an electron, a sub atomic particle is just a
    speck
And so on and on and on forever

However, comparisons do not determine meaning and
"Just" is not demeaning
A speck is sufficient and significant and magnificent!
And all is all
And each is all
And all is each
And that is magical and mysterious and most of all
It is very good!

Holons within holons
All the way down and
All the way up
All interdependent

Without parts there would be no wholes
Without wholes there would be no parts

The same can be said of time
Without the present there would be no past or future
Without the past there would be no present or future
Without the future there would be no past or present

All is one
All is interdependent
Everything is also just itself and
All is just Itself

Space-wise, each thing constitutes and is
All space
Time-wise, every moment constitutes and is
All time
-F L O W I N G –
          D A N C I N G –

Everything and every time is flowing
Changing, becoming, letting go, transforming
I live in the universe; I am the universe
The universe lives in me; the universe is me
I live in all time; I am all time
All time lives in me; all time is me
I am 13 billion years old and will live as long
As The universe lives!
Hooray for me! Hooray for the universe!
I love the universe; and the universe loves me!

I am forever
Forever is me
I am all in all
All in all is me
And there is only
The Dance!

EVERY DAY IS EARTH DAY

Every day is Earth day
and always has been
the only place we
have ever known a day
or night or anything
else at all
these years, four billion,
two million, 200,000,
5,000, twenty fourteen
hooray for our heavenly
home, beautiful beyond
beauty, alive beyond
aliveness, abundant
for all
and yet, and yet
we humans divide and
hoard and pillage and rape
and harm our mother,
our own body;
but now is waking up time
making up time
time to cherish and conserve
for the next 1,000, million,
billion years or so
yes
let's

EARTHLING VOWS

Earth, our only home
Precious beyond priceless
Gift of the universe
Our mother who gives us life
Earth, our only home
We cherish you and vow
To keep you safe from harm
We swoon at the stunning beauty
Of your land
Earth, our only home
We give you thanks for air and water
We delight in your plants and animals
We celebrate each of your humans
Earth, our only home
We vow to let go of violence and greed
And create a new civilization of
Compassion and understanding
Earth, our only home

IN CELEBRATION OF MT. AVILA

rising above and over and behind
and beyond the human city (called Caracas)
so ever green and high, undulating,
ever changing - browns and greys,
white clouds mist-hidden in the early morn,
dark blue at night, rain-soaked, shocking,
searing Caribbean sun
revealing yet again your countenance
uniting millions in a common perception
of majesty and stability
forcing us to contemplate the
mystery of our planet's violent, vibrant
journey of four billion years.

I delight in your being there
in your shape, your earth-rock-tree-grass body
your being here (and so near)
confronting my sight and sense with
your ambivalent ambiance

my eyes are lifted up to thee
and beyond
to the shining sea
and above to the sky-blue sky
and rising to our moon and onward to our
Star
and catapulted across our galaxy and into
the cosmic immensity
filled with speeding light, vortices of energy,
swirling, singing of love

O magic mountain,
overflowing gratitude bubbles in my heart,
for you connect me
in one sight
to Earth and Cosmos and
most of all to
Mystery.
gracias, montaña de misterio

ONLY THIS

only this
only this
this is sufficient
this is it
this is all
sunshine
the river
neighbors
moving forward
here and now

EARTH HAD A DREAM

Earth had a dream called history
but a flicker, fluttering frames of light –
a few seconds (12,000 years?)
after four billion years of slumber,
a wakeful dream, a dream about
"hominization" –
or was it her-story?

DNA, radiation belts, the I Ching,
a unified resonant field theory,
off and on, binary crossover,
flung from unity-consciousness
into the field of yin and yang,
male and female, God and human,
good and bad, plus and minus,
darkness and light,
blinking, twinkling on and off,
the language of space-time,
history-consciousness –
sprung from cosmic radiation
and shifting tectonics,
and the pulses of civilization,
emergent human
between heaven and earth,
geomancy and holonomics,
the noosphere spun out,
double-helix spinning,
and now
we enter
The Solar Age
Our Star

Energy
for a few more billion years
waking from amnesia
from a pseudo-one-dimensionality
toward the One-without-a-second,
through two-of-a-kind
for now

Psi-bank unfolding, the unconscious,
the archetypes,
vibrational frequencies,
we are all contemporaries,
Gilgamesh and Buddha,
Sister Teresa and Eve,
Moses and Jesus,
Mother Teresa and Hildegard,
Mohammed and Gandhi,
Athena and Margaret,
the computer-of-the-year,
Earth unfolding
her majestic communion of
bacteria,
attunement with the
eternal present,
from her perspective (and his)

the baby cries
the god-man dies
Quetzalcoatl doth arise
and the Virgin smiles
in compassionate radiance

forever

DUCKS SWIMMING IN A ROW

ducks swimming in a row
one by one
is it drudgery or ecstasy
or simply natural?
Is it tyranny or release?
Is it choice?
Conscious, sub-conscious,
Unconscious?
The essence of duckness?
Fun or boring?
A way to get from here to there?
A ritual, exercise or parade?
A display of "here we are"
"getting all your ducks in a row"
    is not so difficult if
    you are a lead duck!
That is if you have those who
    Will follow
Or perhaps it is "being in a line"
    That is important and not
    Following or leading at all

A GIFT GIVEN

All the earth
belongs to all
the people
and living beings
that populate this
spinning ball
our planet
who else could so
claim it
except the rightful
heir
born of its soil
nurtured by its air
sustained by its waters
engaged in its toil
filled with its sights
and smells and tastes
and touched by its sorrow
awakened by its suffering
caring for its rivers and fields
longing for its life
in its fulness
God-given communion
co-creating
here and now its history

Cultures born of ecstasy
religions born of mystery
ecosystems born of adapting
cities born of complexity

nations born of tradition
languages born of joy and terror
sexes born of union
diversity and separation (glory or curse?)
the cosmic order
yet one earth only
one humanness evolved
one past and
one future
ours
we are one
in spite of our manyness
reconciled
a gift given
received celebrated adored

Knowing that you know
what you know
- consciousness —
ecstatic union of
substance-form-and-mind
one experience
ours only (all sentient ones)
our burden
to bear
for this exquisite universe
as its eyes its ears its voice
its Song of
thank you for
what was, is and is to be
YES

HUDSON RIVER MOMENTS

i.
rain falling gently
lightning flashes
a distant rumble
once again
night overtakes
the Hudson Valley

ii.
Still as glass
The river reflects
The gray sky
Misty mountains
On the other shore
Beyond all suffering
We are all there
Now

iii.
The river looks heavy
Like chocolate pudding
With whipped cream
Waves and peaks
The wind, mud and water,
Flowing together in
Choppy harmony
A dance of ultimate expression

iv.
Morning haze covers mountain tops
Calm warm air fills the valley
Gray water ripples, flowing
A sailboat passes slowly
The train rolls toward the city
Acceptance of the Is
Gratitude for all
Eternal Now

v.
Rushing along the riverside
From the marsh to Manhattan
Sunlight plays on the
Hillside
The river runs supreme
Both ways

vi.
Liquid, dancing
Peaks of gray river
Attention
This is it

SPINNING, WHIRLING, EARTH, AND AIR

Spinning, whirling, Earth, and air,
Fire, water, we are all of it, it is us

THE DIVINE COMEDY: NO JOKE

What is the Divine Comedy?
Is it God's joke on us humans?
We are born, become conscious of all space and all time,
and then we die.
What is it all about – this life and death?
In this vast Cosmos do we matter at all?
I like to think we do.
We are the Cosmos come conscious.
And that's a lot.
That is amazing.
That is worth being.
No joke.
And in our time and place, can we not love it all,
every creature great and small?
Yes, love is the way, the truth, the light.
Nothing else makes any sense to me whatsoever.
And that means everything.
Let's be our consciousness of this sublime mystery
in humility, gratitude and compassion.
Spiraling, flinging out our star stuff for one and all.

WE ARE A HUMAN BEING FIRST

We are human beings first,
and then we are a sex, a gender, an age, a race,
an ethnicity, a religious conviction, a nationality,
a political persuasion, a sexual orientation,
an economic class, an educational level.
No, actually we aren't a human being first.
First we are part of this mysterious Cosmos,
then we are part of the Milky Way,
then the solar system,
then the living Earth,
then we are an animal,
a mammal,
then we are hominids,
and THEN we are human beings.
We do have a lot in common with all of our
sisters and brothers, yes?
And what is this family resemblance?
Each of us emerged from what had come before
We each change continually
We are interdependent in co-origination
We are empty of a separate self
We each grow old and pass away
And thus we shout out:
Solidarity!
Love!
Mystery!

FOR W.I.T.

(in honor of William Irwin Thompson)

for what was said
was heard as well
a mouthful.
an earful
mind-fully present
and who presents
and who receives
the presents
an ecology of mind
fully operative
here and now
(forever?)
for what is
is what thought gives
and is for now
here
for us
as us
is us

a poetry of cosmos
logos
words strung out
upon a page or
read aloud
and heard
but what of
action and a
style of life

yes
what of them
and all the rest
is it enough
and even is it
it or not an it at all
but all or nothing
grounded here and now
and what of this or is it
this or that or not at all
or here or now or then or there
but with us
in us
as us
is us
or not
but for you; decide and do
and know and be
or not at all
yes.

THE STILL POINT AT THE CENTER

The still point at the center of
   Swirling change
The dervish spins but
   Remains at the still point

FOR MY COLLEAGUES OF THE WAY

for the way is narrow and
many are they who are called but few chosen
- by themselves, by the Self -
selfless, self-negating,
self-actualizing, self-fulfilling,
you who are among the few,
give thanks for your being,
your burden, your blessing,
your broken heart
- sacred and wounded -
by love, by tragedy, by the
suffering of your neighbor

listen and hear the song of becoming
- transforming -
dying, being reborn anew
again and again
and again

the pattern has been let loose
on this planet
the process is out
the rhythm is throbbing, alive
- awake -
for your sake and for all who
take up the singing within and without
and who are about

the one knowing,
the one doing,
the one being,
in a unique, precious manifestation
- you -

DOMINGO

the black curtain - of Mystery
to accept death
the incense - of Mystery
to receive life
the bells - of Mystery
to worship God
the chanting - of Mystery
to celebrate the Final Unknownedness
the songs - of Mystery
to stand at attention
the flames - of Mystery
to contemplate the One Without a
Second

tears flowing
there is no why
there is only
I AM

POEM #201287.2

cosmos sound and sight
music, fireworks, BANG – ing,
hearing, playing, resounding,
resonance, remembering,
and light and warmth and
speech, to each, dialogically,
a logic all its own,
majesty, dignity, awesome mystery
galaxies born of dust and gas and
light
energy that is love
stars exploding into sight and
sound and space and time
spinning, swirling, swimming,
yearning, reaching,
beseeching,
a plaintive flute -
rising and falling
Pachelbel's Canon
so much, much more dignity,
flowing, inter-weaving of
hope, faith and love,
O to dance,
a chance to be
this one
now and here
forever, heretofore
evermore

amor, amor, amor,
and shadow, meadow
doe and deer
and do or die
an eye or my, I, aye

GNIEB

being your being, being my being, then
everything will flow, flow
through you, with you, and what of
discipline,
interior or external, fear of energy,
fear of flowing, flying, letting go,
dying, changing, transforming,
to die is to live is still
the truth about Life
and what of now, and how,
for what and why and when and
for whom
Room for More
Adoration of Being

THE SEARCH IS ENDED

a life of love
of music,
dance,
of resonance within fields of
pure energy
of meditation, contemplation and prayer
of service, work, action,
energy in motion
a sourcing at the Source
a system,
process,
a rhythm of both/and, and much,
much more,
a dialogue
a coming and a going
a life with
the Beloved of the Soul

FOR NOW

the wind,
whence cometh?
where goeth?
it blows where it will
and when, Gaia's breath,
inhaling and exhaling,
from a centeredness
of 4 billion years

I faint, my head spins,
will I fall?
where am I?
who am I?
transformation is not
for the weak and
who are you?
he asks
from Olympian heights
of power
ego, I go, vertigo, a while ago,
all aglow,
for the show,
no,
for the story

fascination of a
child of a
nation of children,
we who are waiting,
for the now to

burst with its
pregnant eternity
the already,
sound, but is it,
and what of sight,
and all the rest and
which is best

forget me not
O fellow travelers
on the way
but forget
the way it could
have been
for fear a pillar
of salt
thou may become
come and be
maybe or maybe not

POEM #211287

O ecstasy of sacred sound
whence cometh Bach's B Minor Mass
around the arched cathedral space
alas shines forth the Holy Face

Triumphant strains flame out within
and I become the one without
a name

THE PRECIOUS GIFTS

You can only know healing
If you are sick
You can only know reunion
If you are separate
You can only know power
If you are weak
You can only know fullness
If you are empty

Isn't this what Shakyamuni Buddha meant
When he said, "All is suffering"
Did he not mean "Healing is possible
Happiness is possible,
Peace is possible"

Isn't this what Jesus Christ meant
When he said, "Blessed are the poor
In Spirit
For they shall see God
Blessed are the hungry
For they shall be fed
Blessed are the last
For they shall be first"

Isn't this what the theologian meant
When he said, "When you are at the
End of your rope, then you can
experience
Being accepted by a power greater than
you"

When we become aware of our suffering
Then we can realize nirvana
When we become aware of our
separation
Then we can experience reunion
When we become aware of our weakness
Then we can feel great power
When we become aware of our emptiness
Then we can be filled with everything

Thanks be for these most precious gifts
The gift of suffering
The gift of the awareness of suffering
The gift of the healing of suffering
The gift of a life of happiness and peace

THE WORD: THIS IS IT!

Waiting.
Longing.
When will someone or something come to make it all okay?
When will someone arrive to transform our situation so that we can truly live, fully live?
Waiting for so long.
Longing for so much.
And what appears is a helpless babe who grows in wisdom and love and is executed by the state at the age of 33.
This one who kept the company of prostitutes and tax collectors, who threw out the money changers, who said love your enemies, surely this cannot be the one for whom we have been waiting and longing. But if it were, what is the message we hear and know?
"Don't wait any longer.
No one else is coming.
The fullness of time is now.
We can live and love our lives fully here and now just as they are."
This message is good and great news indeed, that we can live our given lives, our real situations as a gift, in humility, in gratitude, in compassion, in ecstasy.
Yes, this is good news beyond anything we could ever expect or anticipate.
This is it!
All-that-is is good and perfect!

You, just as you are, are accepted and sustained in mystery!
The past, just as it is, is received by history!
The future is wildly open for you to co-create!
Hallelujah!
Hallelujah!
Hallelujah!

AND THEY SET FORTH
— A PILGRIMAGE POEM —

And some heard the Cry, and set forth
    Others saw the Vision, and set forth
Some felt the Pulse, and set forth
    Others tasted the Nectar, and set forth
And still others smelled the Aroma, and set forth.

the one who converses with Athena and the Black shaman
    the compassionate judge and the transparent nurse
the passionate teachers and the ones who cherish the
homeless
    the monk who makes drums and the communicator
of stories
the one who makes images and the archetypal elder
    the one who plays her heart-string and the Latino
sage
the planetary Texan-ecumenical Baptist and the ones
who awaken
    executives to spirit
    the People of the Question, the Actress, and Dorothy
They set forth.

They set forth in boldness, on a sacred pilgrimage
    the inward dromenon within the outward journey
They set forth in courage, toward Century 25
    with the gods and goddesses, they set forth
to weave, to see, to touch the unknown unknown,
    to dream the dream of becoming,
with gold bursting from the center,

led by a Vision of The Living Book of the Second Genesis
They set forth
with their Beloved Archetypes
    They set forth.

Into fractal wave patterns, morphic resonance,
the Very Mind of God
    They set forth.

With peace pipe, the animals, the children, Margaret
and Teilhard,
    they set forth.

Toward Type One — High Level Civilization, they set
forth,
    Down through the Sensory to the Psychological, to
the Mythic
and the Unitive - to find the sacred gift - to return to
this world
empowered — to serve — to cherish the uncherishable.

And now they set forth to the birthplace of the Great
Liberator,
    to the shrines of the two Maria's, to the land of the
Caribbean-Andes-Amazon—Yanomami-Orinoco-
llanos—joropo-Barlovento-
    the shining white City - the land full of energy - a
people
full of energy, a people, once liberated, now struggling
to build
    the New Venezuela

See!
- the brilliant green parrots taking flight, joined by the
yellow ones - filling the sapphire sky in the blazing tropi-
cal sun

Hear!
- the harp being strummed, plucked, tickled

Taste!
— *arepa, hayaca, papaya, guayanaba* - so sweet

Feel!
— the hot sand, the cool breeze, the sun-blasts, the rocky
path under your feet

Smell!
- the fish, the fragrant flowers, the sour cacao, the
incense

You are there — now, here — then
Yes — us — we - all - one
One land from South to North
Our home
One People of The New World.

A m e r i c a n s !

who speak Spanish—English—Portuguese-French-
Dutch
Yes - all that and much, much more.

We celebrate our past and we claim our future
for The New Earth,
a new way of bringing forth a world together,
a planetary ecology of cultures,
a New Civilization, a new hope, a new song
a New Dance.
We set forth!

APPRECIATING BOTH PROCESS AND RESULTS
(for a UN workshop)

People are suffering
The earth herself groans with
too-muchness
Why are we here?
What is our role - to create or destroy?

My mission is to live with integrity
To make a difference in other people's lives
To respect individual, gender and cultural differences
There is real pride and joy when I see results

How do we make a difference in peoples' lives?
How be one program, one team?
How deal with vested interests?

Is development a symphony or jazz?
How do we change at the speed of the imagination?
If words create reality, we must be very careful what we
     say
Perhaps the key is not an answer but a question, a dia-
     logue, an image, an expectation
How respond to Einstein's challenge to move to another
     level of consciousness?
How shift from doing to being?
How make for a happier life for all beings?
Systems matter but we appreciate that people matter
     more

Isn't it really all about love?
It is so simple
We make it so complex, with
too many words, systems, frameworks
Let us breathe in sweet air
Let us embrace one another
Let us shake off our ancient prejudices and
build the earth
We are all connected and interdependent
Separation is an illusion

Remember:
- The great tree, the termites and Jack and the
golden beans
- The bridge across the lake
- The kaleidoscope and the dialogue between the UN
    and the
countries
- One common system for development
effectiveness
- The one UN dance
- The clever hero octopus with the sexy tentacles in
the hydroplane
- The crayon Picasso with a hot sun, big drops
of rain and a rainbow of people, dogs and
elephants
- That the SG is our leader, but we are not a
monolithic organization
- That we must increase our efforts to help the most
vulnerable
- That we need to revisit afresh UNDP's relationship
to program countries

There is only change
How flow with it?
How dance with it?
How be present to it?
This beautiful blue-green marble spinning, soaring
through space
This is our home
We are one family
May all beings be happy
May all beings be at peace
May all beings be compassionate
May all beings be wise
So be it
Be it so.

A MYTHIC JOURNEY
(The New Vision of the House of Wainwright)

Isolated - in house, in heart, in hope
    We came
Not knowing, open, expectant
    We set forth

Into the gray stone mansion by the Sound
    We entered
To a sacred place, to the source, to the center
    We returned

On a vision quest
    We set forth
To a bright-eyed lady of passion
    Together we came

Forming as a circle of friends
    a circle of unity
We danced the dance of deep recognition
    "I have known thee of old"
We adjourned to a provincial salon

We journeyed to ancient Epidaurus where we
    Laughed, we cried, we sang, we danced,
We were enlivened by comedy, deepened by tragedy
    By philosophy we were called forth
We were touched and we touched others
    Reaching out to the god-in-hiding

O Asclepios! Heal and whole us so that
   We might whole and heal many others!
And the god stretched out his/her hand and
   We were touched

We dreamed the dream of the healing and
   Wholing of our beloved community
Our courageous leader dared to dream the
   Dream in the sacred tomb before the
   Sacred altar where he slept to
   Dream the dream of becoming

   We entered the center of the temple
      Patches of dark and light
   To the center for contact
      Bringing gifts
   We knelt down
      Competitiveness vanished,
   Love was born
      A fountain sprang forth
   A large eye appeared
      A dragon flowed into the temple
   The cosmic human, the city on the hill
      Energy in the heart of
   Compassion

   Of this we dreamed

When we awoke we ascended the staircase
To the sacred altar, the ancient tree,
Placed in our charge by the solitary saint
And there, in the empty mandala-space,
We invoked the Spirit, who spoke with many

Voices, with words of vision and
Courage, we spoke and were silent in
Gratitude

Then we journeyed on and up the steep slope
    Of a mountain to the very top and
Into and down through four gates leading to
    Four realms of
        The Senses
            The Psyche
                The Symbol, and
                    The One-without-a-second
To be gifted by a great being
    We returned up the interior of
The mountain with our giftedness
    We returned to the light of day
With our gifts - so many gifts!
    A scroll of wisdom to pass to youth
    A teaching plant for warriorship
    Enough for everyone
    Creativity and receptivity
    Trust, inner knowing and
        Vulnerability
    Heart touching heart
    With shadows released
Then we saw the Light behind the Shadow
We saw the unique gift in the
        Shadowy struggle
Behind the Shadow of Power we saw it -
    The Gift of a Center of Power!
A sacred site, a psychic magma,
    A fertile place of immense energy

Rising before us we saw the Vision!
    Sparkling and radiant we saw it

We saw a great wheel turning
At the center of the wheel we saw
    A Flame and the keepers of the
    Flame, listening to the
    Spirit, a small band of
    Deepened and extended
    Beings
And around this flame we saw a
    Center of healing and wholing
        An Asclepian center - a
        Power Center - empowering
        People through performance,
        Art, expressive therapia
    And radiating out from the center
We saw three spokes of the wheel
    Servant leadership to the
        Least, the last and the lost
    A School for Social Artistry
        Reinventing sociality,
        Polity, economics, culture,
        New forms and methods of
        Becoming the social beings
        We are, and
    An Institute of Thought, with
        People reflecting deeply,
        Breaking new ground, on the
        Cutting edge, modeling,
        Spinning out sapiential
        Circles across the land
But this Vision was really only

One - a social passion feeding the
Inner flame which feeds the
Social passion, the within-and—the
Without, a sacred, transforming power

And we agreed to agree, to commit, to attract,
    To seek, to find, to fund, to learn, to share,
To be a micro-society of deep inner training, and
    Outer expression, of
Community and Communion
    We agreed to hold the pattern in the view of
Three full moons, in order to
    Convince the universe of our sincerity and
Our earnestness
    We agreed to explore and to honor
        Traditional beliefs,
            Personal growth, and
Social harmony

We celebrated the gods within and without
    We celebrated our multiple selves
We celebrated our modeling of the future
    The leading edge,
We stepped into tomorrow and next week
    Into next year and we returned
With heart-felt resolve
    We thanked the bright-eyed lady of passion
Who had graced us with laughter and with
    Possibility

    This is no winter now
        The human heart can go to the lengths of

G O D

These are the times and
  We are the people,
The People of the House of
  Wainwright.

SENTIMENTS ON A BLUE AND GOLD CUB SCOUT

Richard was the purple patch of Horace Mann
    to which he often wore blue-jeans
    with both knees patched in blue

His thick blond third-grade hair fell down
    in healthy locks to blow and swirl
    on windy winter days at noon recess

His wide-eyed third-grade face was set
    with blue-blue eyes which never ceased
    to sparkle and take in the world
    til he was home and mother kissed him
    off to sleep

Richard was the purple patch of Horace Mann
    and all his teachers loved this blue-gold boy
    who ran in little canvas-white and rubber
    tennis shoes to play and wave his strong
    young arms and yell and whistle at the birds
    and sky and trees to climb and brooks to wade
    and third-grade dreams to dream

But even blue-gold boys grow up

Richard won the purple heart when he was
twenty-one
    for being kissed and put to sleep on Asian soil
    but only after he had shot and killed someone
    or two of Asia's brown-brown boys with thick black
healthy locks that wildly swirled on windy winter days
    above the sparkle of brown eyes

And even while sweet Richard died he held most dear
his third-grade dreams of play and birds and trees
and brooks and all the other things that third-grade
blue-gold boys and brown-brown boys dream of.

PEACE, YES!

Cold could not stop us
Gathering, marching, together we walked
United for peace, against war
United for people, against violence
Americans together speaking out
Emotions swelling, yes, it is possible
We can make a difference
We can invent a better world for all
Yes!

WAR IS TERRORISM

Terrorism mistranslated as "war"
Although war has always brought terror

Barbarism, the most primitive instinct
Of the human animal
Or more precisely of the
Male ego – warrior and killer, driven by
Hormones and emotion and the
Comradeship of other males
Dying for that which is greater
Uniting with the Great Cause
Becoming one with Life and Death
A tragically flawed mysticism

And for what?
Oil? Democracy? Disarmament? Freedom?
Righteousness? Empire? Corporate contracts?

Such heartbreak
To see our precious, soft
Baby boys and girls grow up to
Maim and kill other babies, women, men
Who were once soft and precious
Held in their mother's arms
Now cold and hard
And to be maimed or die themselves

May our hearts grow ever larger to give space to
Everyone
May a mother's love rise within

Each of us
May we tame and transcend our little egos
May we give up war for
Wisdom, and carnage for compassion

AUTUMN VIEW

Red, gold, brown
Yellow and green
Swirling, filling the sky
The river reappears
The mountain emerges
In all its thereness
Two birds fly northwest
The ground, the path,
The fruition
In a single glance
All one

Silver canisters
Rain from the blue sky
Desert dust fills the air
Red wetness soaks the sand
A limb spins in the
Morning sun
Landing on five clenched
Fingers
In a single glance
A flood of tears
All one

I AM SICK, BUT . . .

I am sick
Sick of war
The sad suffering
Families running from danger
Blood, injury, death and destruction

I am sick
Sick of the glorification of war
The media hype
As if war were macho and sexy
As if it were a football match
With winners and losers

I am sick
Sick that my own country is the
Aggressor
That my government prefers bombs
To health care
Prefers dominance to diplomacy
Prefers bullying and bribery over
Mutual respect and listening

I am sick
Sick that humanity is still so
Primitive that we must kill those
With whom we disagree
That young people are still trained
To be professional killers
That war is seen by many as a legitimate activity

I am sick
Sick at heart, but I vow to
Wage peace that is sexier, more
Attractive and livelier than any war

COLLECTION TWO

Poems Commemorating Family and Self

GRAND MOTHER DUNCAN

Sally Ann to some
to others - Mother
Grand Mother to me
slender when I knew her
silver hair always up and
neatly arranged
The Lady
even in the evenings when it
gently fell to her shoulders
Gracious
dark deep set eyes
fullness of mouth
quiet of speech
always The Lady

I remember stories
of the early days
wagons west horseback pistols
broom corn and a little oil
selling cottona young family
in Oklahoma

A Christian Lady
church and Sunday school
Gentleness of spirit
alert to the suffering of this world
yet GenerousTrusting

a quiet house
white frame

green grass flowers a swing
a porch looking out on second avenue
when the world was going mad
a sanctuary of stillness and calm

sharing her life with others
caring for so many daily hourly
symbolizing love
A Lovely Lady

I am proud and grateful
for your life

THREE-FOLD KINDNESS PRAYER

I regret my unkindness to others
I am grateful for the kindness I receive
I vow to manifest kindness toward all beings

MARY

How can I
say it (no weary words)
the one who had to be
mine
with me
everywhere for
every time to
talk to plan to argue,
you strange one
the one to love
- the other -
the dialogue for doing
a deed
history changing,
being a pioneer
in the ghetto and the
village
standing with the poor
living fully
fulfilling life's promise
of joy and sorrow
in covenant with
all, symbolized with
one
once and for all
we
far flung or known
creating, inventing the
new now, here
what more to do

ecstasy and issue
we three, four
together
a journey
a sign
a path opened up
this way!
follow us
this way!
audacious indicative
hooray!

A FAMILY TRANSPARENCY:
SON'S ADOPTION POEM

I.
Selfhood in faith
Marriage with hope
Children as love

Simply
Parents without children
Children without parents
Adoption creates
A family
The family of people
The family of God
We are all children of God by
Adoption, whereby we cry
Ababa! Father! Mother!
Like Abraham and Sarah
Waiting those many years
Nevertheless
Nothing
But the
Decision
which births resolve
Which nurtures action
which emboldens the
Faint-hearted
My God my God
Why what when where who
How

Our fate here and now
In this strange land
Is our destiny
Yes yes yes
And then
God plays a joke
On us

For our own good
Fruitfulness!
Nature really works!
Nevertheless
Decision is more powerful
Than accident
Not sentiment
No liberalism
Only brokenness, a tragedy
Made whole in
Deciding it is
For you

The stone the builders
Rejected, God has made the
Corner stone
In fear and trembling
Yet knowing
That no right conclusion
Awaits around the turn
Only the way -- the Tao
Not as a problem to be
Solved, but a Mystery
To be lived
We set out

II.
In humiliation and weakness
With hostility and suffering
We set out
The Great Adventure
Sheer risk

And yet in
Mystery
With care
In entire freedom
And with unbounded joy
We set out

Destiny is always
Here and now
Deciding for the
Given as the good
Indicating imperative
To dare to
Care for
Today
And tomorrow
Incarnate significance
Beyond primordial boundaries
Re-union with the other
ever Present
The morrow in tension
Intentionally
Ecstatic
In mundanity of
Diapers
Demonstrating agape

The greatest of these
is here and now
Forever
With us
For us

LOVE

Male
Female
Child
Profound
Mundanity
Of creaturehood
Living care fully
For the morrow
In overflowing
Significance
Thank you thank you thank you
For what is
For what matters is
Spirit
The really real
What matters is
What is and
Must-will be
Being a creature
As creation's glory to God
The full catastrophe

III.
And of this one
Only intention
Only love
A sacramental sign
To civilization
Gone global
Aflame within the
Real unknown
The unknown unknown

From grassy plain
And arid desert
From jagged mountain
They emerge
Be ye not offended!
The child of tomorrow's man
with Buddha's yellow face
And Plato's brain
And the spirit of this
Blue planet
A new heart-beat
A throw of the dice
On which rests the entire
Future
Come and go with us
To this land
That is here and now
Forever.

BENJAMIN

My pride
mystery man
found— chosen-
destiny— necessity
ours- us
laughing smiling one
my brown-eyed boy
hair shiny black
straight so straight
my son
a face
so round so round
dimples two
you
who loves to study
to save, to succeed
and does it all
who are you?
brown—yellow boy
who knows suffering
and joy and all the rest
(lost and found)
in the city or the village
North or South
East or West
you love it
You I love-
citizen of the world
child of a global village

CHRISTOPHER

Yellow hair
down straight
some gold some brown
green eyes-
little boy who likes math
long arms long legs
running bare foot
up a village path
with your Black friends
my son
I love you

Grow grow grow
be a better man, one
who knows
the sorrow of
poverty and the delights
of simplicity (and
jet flights and video games)
who are you?
golden-white boy
who knows patois
who grew up in a
Korean—Comanche—Jamaican
village
I love you-
citizen of the world-
child of a global village

WHERE ARE YOU?

Mary,
It is so quiet without you.
It is so still.
Where is your boundless
Energy?
Where is your quick
Mind?
Where is your strong
Voice?
Where is your tall
Presence?
Your cheer?
Your warmth?

Now, we must look within our
Hearts to find you.
We must look at everyone and
Everything to find you.
You are everywhere, but
We must look, carefully.
We must listen, expectantly.
Then we will find you every time.
Laughing with us.
Loving us.
Guiding us.

Thank you, for
Your love.
Always.

DECIDE AND CHOOSE

Sickness
Nightmares
He said that she said
It will always be a tragedy
I don't agree
Chris doesn't either
It is life
In its mystery
It is our job to accept

Sixty one years is not 71 or 81
but it is also not
51, 41, 31 or 21
How long is enough?
Only Mary and her God
Could decide
We must accept in
Gratitude
We must live in
Gratitude

But as for me,
What about it?
What now?
Who am I without
My partner?

The river is gray
The highlands in mist
Ripples dance lightly

What next?
Chris says the old
Journey is over
I don't want to hear
No, I cry out within
I don't want it to be over
Chris says that I must
Decide what I want
He has said before that
I deserve to be happy
Mary would want that
She would say, get on
With living!
Love your life!
I am gone
But with you still
In the stillness of your heart
But look around
Decide
Go for it!

I feel weak and sick
I want to withdraw
But I must go on
And choose or
Be chosen.

DEATH IS NOT A SURPRISE, NOT A FAILURE

Death is not a surprise, not a failure,
　　Not a mistake
It is part of life. It is a transition –
　　A trans-form-ation.
It awakens our compassion for
　　All beings, including myself.
Because of death, each being is
　　Infinitely precious, each
Moment is infinitely precious
　　Death reminds us of what
Is important – what is lasting.
　　Material objects pass away.
Spirit is the Really Real.
　　Love is eternal.
Life is forever.

A LADY WITH A RED ROSE

A lady with a red rose
Fog on the river
Moment by moment
Surprise after surprise
In continuity
Rising and falling
A flow onwards
Impermanence in motion
Overlapping eddies of energy

Warm fog
Empty fog
Empty warmth
Empty self
Effulgence in the four directions

HILLSIDE COTTAGE

Hidden by the mountain
yet open to the sky
Nestled in the valley
yet seeing the river
Rooted in this world
yet a doorway to the other
Calm and serene
yet sparkling and fiery
A place for humans
yet full of wild animals
Made of wood and stone
yet it does not exist
Fully formed
yet fully empty
No hill and no cottage
only all space and time
Flowing onwards

LIFE IS FOR THE LIVING

Why did he say?
Let the dead bury the dead
Is it not the lot of the living
To go on with living
Never missing a beat
Seeing the beauty of a
Flower or a sunset
Smelling the freshness of
Rain or a baby after its bath
Planning, enjoying, eating,
Talking, helping, serving
But always knowing that this
Is not all
There is more
There is the absolute unknown
There is the cloud of witnesses
All those who once lived
All those we still love
And who still love us
Waiting, surrounding us,
Permeating everything,
Expectantly
Pregnant with union
With the divine.
Does this not make our day
More precious
Each person
Glorious
Calling us to life fully
While yet alive?

LIVE AND DIE FULLY

Death is so final
So ultimate
So unyielding
Gone, gone, completely gone
Where and what
We know not
Only mystery, sheer and
Impenetrable
Absolute unknownness
Only trust and go on
Accept and be grateful
For your life
For her life
For our life
For Life everlasting
Flowing onwards
Forever
World with end
Amen

Contemplate my death
Breathe it in and out
And no more
Become intimate with
My death
My dead body
My goneness
My not hereness
My mysterious departure
Accept it

Live it
Don't fear it
Love it

Live fully
Live once
As this one
No doubts
Abandonment
Do it all, now
Love it with every
Movement and voice
Dance it in
Ecstasy
Yes!

GOING TO MANHATTAN ONCE AGAIN

going to Manhattan once again
and for the first time

MARY, I LOVE YOU STILL

But love is eternal
And life is forever
Even in death
No separation
Only all in all
One

Thank you, my love
For gracing us with
Your presence
Thank you for your love
Presenting us with
Grace daily
35 years was sufficient
But not enough

You said
We mustn't be greedy
You said
I am so grateful for my life
You let go in perfect surrender
You are now one with the
Endlessness of Mystery

Thank you, my love
Your love continues
Strong and full
My love for you grows

My broken heart bleeds
Compassion for all

I love you forever
Even unto the endless end

MY WIFE, MY LIFE

Form is emptiness
Emptiness, form
Appearance emerging
Seemingly from nothing
Although already present
From beginningless beginning
Present, changing, growing, declining
Suddenly still, frozen, burning
Ash, scattered
Apparently gone, merged
Nothing left save everything
What apparently wasn't, was
What apparently was, isn't
But always was and always will be
Unto endless end
As endless mystery
Always present, ever absent
Empty, yet fullness overflowing
Gratitude, the only response

PRAYER

Mary,
My Life Partner,
Who is in the Other World
In the midst of This World,
Blessing, honor and love be
Yours this day and forever.
May the Realm of Goodness
Be manifest more and more.
May the Realm of Truth
Be articulated increasingly
In This World as well as in
The Other World within This World.
May all beings be happy
This day.
And may we do no harm,
And experience communion with
All beings.
And may we respond with
Loving kindness to those who
Do us harm.
And protect us from negative
Thoughts and actions.
In your angelic name, as
Well as in the name of
Mary, the Mother of God,
Kwan Yin, the Bodhisattva of
Compassion, and
The Endless Mystery

In the midst of and beyond
All that is and is not
Be it so
So be it

EVERYTHING THAT COMES TO BE

Everything that comes to be
    Passes away
Or seems to
Actually that which seems
To come to be was always
Present
And that which seems to
Pass away
Is also present
    Eternally
The endless flowing
    The measureless ocean
The all in all
    And yet
There will never be another
    You

THEY SET OUT

They set out
From Westchester
From Korea, Oklahoma, Jamaica,
From Venezuela, they set out
Across a vast land, to see, to know,
To discover themselves, to uncover a
Future of possibility
Embodying generations of love
With questions, with hopes, with
Dreams
They set out
With youthful energy
With deep concerns
With hard work
They set out
Filled with skills, with knowledge,
With talents, with capacities
They set out
To touch, to hear, to smell, to taste
The Suchness of what is
To STOP, relax
Reflect and write
To invent, to decide, to take a
Direction
On behalf of themselves
On behalf of all

Be safe, be happy, enjoy!
Return refreshed and invigorated to
Create a future

THE VISION QUEST

A sacred journey
Across a sacred land
Two lovers on a
Vision quest
To family and friends
To places known and unknown
Exploring futures
Inventing a life
Making the possible real

Enjoy, be open, relax,
Nothing can go wrong with your trip
What happens was meant to be
Just be

Struggles there will be
Surprises, turns in the road
Continuing on into the known and unknown
You go
Be safe, travel well,
Return refreshed and charged with a
Future coming to be

On behalf of family, friends,
Even the whole world
You go out through day and night
New vistas, new thoughts,

New people, new possibilities
I pray for your happiness and
Fulfillment
Be it so

DANCING ON WATER

dancing on water
  trusting life to uphold us
  a consistency of enthusiasm
  O, beautiful bodhisattva
  radiate your compassion on
  all beings everywhere
  thank you for being here
  thank you for your love
  thank you for your poetry
  thank you for your teaching
  stay a long time
  practice the great perfection
  be joy, dance
  for it is all good
  yes!

CLOUDS WHITE

Clouds white
Sky blue
Faded prayer flags flutter
Green branches swaying

Light fills my eyes
Looking out
Feeling inward

What is love?
Not just for this or that one
But for all life

So precious, fleeting
Here, gone
Sorrow fills the void

Deep breath
Stillness
Silence

HEART OF LOVE

I am crazy for you
wild about you
you beautiful being
you sexy thing
you wild woman
you who are mad
    for truth,
you who embody
    love
I love your body
    all of it
All round and
    smooth
Hot and cool
every bit outside and
    inside
I love your mind
    all of it
All vast and poetic
Fiery and calm
every thought and
    feeling
I love your spirit
    all of it
All empty and full
Wild and silent
every intention and
    gesture
How can I live
    without you

Thank you for
  becoming my
  neighbor,
  the bowl of
  soup,
  the talk,
  the walk,
  the deep
  embrace
Thank you for the
  sheets of gold,
  the rose,
  the candle,
  your cushion in
  my heart
Thank you for this
  dreamy dance
May we never wake up
  as we ever awake

TWO LOVERS

i.
two lovers churning through the night
two poets playing ping pong with words
two hermits trying to figure out when to be
alone and when together

ii.
what started it
was it the dharma talks, the picture
was it kwan yin, was it mary
was it Garrison, sesshin
was it tea that turned into dinner
was it the wooden bowls of hot soup
the French kiss, the garlic shrimp
was it the look, the challenge to be
never ending presence

iii.
I renounce renunciation
say no to celibacy
I am no monk

iv.
our intimacy is the most
precious thing in my life
I know that we are called to intimacy with
The ten thousand things
That is true

But this is truer still
Just one, only one
And through her all the rest

v.

be patient my love
be strong
forgive
taste happiness without end

vi.

if I still loved a cloud
that I fell in love with in
1968
wouldn't that be silly
when there are new clouds
every micro second
and yet I will never forget
or stop loving that beautiful cloud

vii.

tiger girl, poet, high priestess
movie star, hermit, lover, enigma
try as I might
I can't stop loving you

viii.

and what am I to you
why can't I accept your love
and what are you to me
a lover, teacher,

bodhisattva
why can't I accept that
I love you

ix.
may your suffering be relieved
may your hurt go away
may you find the place that has
never known suffering
may all doubts dissolve
may all anger subside
may you be happy now and
forever

x.
the conversation continues
with shattered cup and spilt tears,
fears and hiccups
comings and goings
longings and realizations
tenderness and rage
silence and stillness
how to give each other what
the other needs
forgiveness, honesty,
returning to presence
again and again
but more is called for
more is possible
a container is needed
a new cup to hold it all

TEN KISSES

i.
blank void mist
world of white
mountain faintly appearing
chalky forests
gray river
warm inside

ii.
still, so still
tiny flakes of snow
falling
ever so softly
s l o w l y

iii.
practicing missing you
halfmoon eyes, so blue
missing part of myself
where am I?
who am I
without you?

iv.
gold, pure gold
falling gently around
a little ear
a nibble
a kiss, a lick
delicious

neck, throat
lips and
much, much more

v.

dusk falls once more
but for the first time
here
lights appear across
the river
so still gray blue white
snow on a brown branch
tomorrow far away
yesterday gone
just now

vi.

my white-toed cat
wants food, my touch
my love

vii.

dancing in the kitchen
feeding the cat
I feel that
tonight I will run
outside in the snow
naked
and throw myself down
in the deepest drifts
and make love to you

viii.
this feeling in my
stomach
my groin
the tension
the attention
the intention
may they never
go away

ix.
just spoke with you
breathless
sultry
voice

x.
darkness outside
but inside glowing embers
reflections in the window
outside and inside mix,
trade places
I am here but no
I am there with you
holding your hand
walking on the beach

ENGAGEMENT POEM

Once upon a time there was
A Buddhist who was really a Judeo-Christian
And a Judeo-Christian who was really a Buddhist
One was a social activist who had become a contemplative
The other was a contemplative who had become
a social activist

When I first saw you
I saw Kannon
As I came to know you
I encountered the mind of
Manjushri, the true one

When you first saw me
Perhaps you saw Manjushri
And as you came to know me
Perhaps you encountered the mind of
Kannon, the compassionate one

In any case both are needed
And each loves the other
Kannon loves Manjushri
Manjushri loves Kannon
Truth and compassion are
A divine couple

Also
Leo loves Pisces and
Pisces loves Leo
Male monkey loves female monkey
Female monkey loves male monkey
They are a divine couple

They are each distinct
Yet in intimacy they are one
Even the relative and the absolute
Seemingly two, are in intimacy One
Enlightenment hail!

On the eve of the
First anniversary
Of our first conversation
I give you this ring
As a symbol of
My love for you
A symbol of
Our engagement and
Commitment to deep conversation
Leading to holy matrimony
Happiness hail!

May we serve the suffering world
Shining the light of mindfulness,
Wholeness and happiness on all beings
May we do this both as individuals and as
a divine couple
Yes!

LIGHTEST OF BLUE

lightest of blue
stripes of white
a bird
green hills
a river
and you
how I love
am obsessed by
you
I ache for us
yes, we are still
here
please forgive
my hurtfulness
please forgive
my pain
please forgive
my confusion
please forgive
my doubt
please believe
in us still
I am not your father
I am not the boy who
hurt you
I am not the old man
I am just this one
so many words
now only action
will remove the doubt

in this our one year
anniversary month
I recall our great love
swelling and crashing
on the shore of our souls
what is at stake?
what is required?
what is possible?
yes, I did it all
yes, I said it all
yes, it is all true
I love you
I asked you to marry
me
you said yes
you asked me to
marry you
I said yes
we are engaged
let the conversation
continue
let love find
a way home

WAVE SWIRLS CLOUDS LIGHT

Wave swirls clouds light
Bubbles curving cresting
Foaming churning
Dolphins come to play
With their beautiful bodies
From Ithaca to Delphi
The heroes sail
In sun, in haze
Rocky mountains rise
Glass reflections, red dress
A round table of friends
A journey with Athena
Yes, life is good

HONEYMOON

Honey moon
Me and my honey
Sun and moon
Moon struck
Honey in the rock
Water moon
Morning Sunshine

I am married
I am married again
I am married for the first time
I have always been married
I am marriage
I am my Beloved's
My Beloved is mine
I am my Beloved
My Beloved is Me
There is no separation
There is only One
There is only Love

I am made new, again
Since the beginning
Of Time and Space
I am always new
Always beginning
Always fresh
Always becoming
Without birth
Without death

I am grateful
I am gratitude
I am love
Thank you for
Loving me
Forever and ever
World without end

A TRIBUTE TO MOTHERS

Giving birth to new life
Nurturing, sustaining, guiding
Releasing, launching, affirming
Love begetting love
A flow onwards
Mother Earth
Mother Tree
Mother Tiger
Mother Eve
My grandmothers,
Sally and Arrie,
My mother, Mary Elizabeth
My children's mother, Mary
My grandchildren's mother, Jennifer
My grandchildren's grandmother, Bonnie
Baby girls who become young women
Who become leaders of our race
Prime Ministers, presidents, priests
CEOs, managers, engineers,
Artists, doctors, astronauts,
Thank you, thank you, thank you
Love upon love
Gratitude upon gratitude
May we each attain Motherhood
Hail!

MY CHRISTMAS EVE BABY

My Christmas eve baby
Born that day in Seoul
When I was 30 years old
Your mother in labor
Shouted "Aye-gu!"
I called the Sacred Heart
Sisters after you arrived.
They shouted "Christ is born!"
You, blond-haired, green
Eyed one, you grew up
Full of energy and joy
You Korean-Jamaican-
Venezuelan-American boy
Who loved math and Spanish
Always at home in the world.
Walking into any room, you see
What isn't working and fix it
You fell in love with a beautiful
Girl in Larchmont, and now
Have two precious children
You are the best son, best
Brother, best father, and best IT
specialist I know
Thank you for caring for so
Many people. I am so proud of
You, a good man, responsible,
And kind. I love you so very
Much and celebrate your birth,
And life, and 44th birthday, and
Wish for you only health and
Happiness now and forever.

THANKSGIVING 2019:
A POEM FOR OUR FAMILY

Gratitude for this day with family
Such warmth of fire, food, and heart
Grateful for each of you, here, now
And all ancestors who have moved on
Let us also be aware of our native
Brothers and sisters who have lived
Here for 10,000 years. We express
Regret, and sadness at the great
Harm our ancestors caused these
Good people while taking their land
We vow to care for all people every
where, as our sisters and brothers
We are grateful for our nearby star
We are grateful for being Earthlings
We are grateful for life, and health,
And happiness, as we celebrate this
Day, vowing to care for all people
Everywhere, our brothers and sisters.
Our family is so fortunate. We have
So much. We have each other. We
Have opportunities. Some people
Have so little. Some have nothing.
Let us vow to care for all people
Everywhere, our sisters and
brothers. So be it. Let us feast!

WOW! POW!

We waited, and waited
Daddy Chris, and Mama Jen
And all the family
Until you were ready,
Then, suddenly, POW!
You were here,
– Phoenix Orion Work –
The bird arising, the hunter,
The one who protects,
With friends, Emma and Honey,
Vivi, the neighbor,
Movement class, Thomas-the-Train,
Lightening McQueen, Legos,
"I have a question", you would ask
Learning at Azalea Mountain,
Reading book after book after book
Ninja Kids Club, and robots
Going to Fernleaf with Reilly
Visiting Seattle and New York,
Oh, how you are loved!
On Fairfax and Fairview
You, who love to read, and
Write books, and make movies,
And computer games,
And love squishy Roo and Lizzie,
Celebrating you, just as you are,
Happy 12, POW!
May you be happy and make
Others happy
WOW-POW!

CELEBRATING YOU

I had to be there for your arrival
And got to hold you in my arms
Mariela Katharine Work -
Our family's first girl in a long time
I remember the first time I saw
Your gaze, so intense, penetrating
And your drawings, so advanced
Your dancing, so free and graceful
Your schools, Azalea and SOLA
Your acting, so real and creative
Your drumming, so energetic
Thank you for appearing on Earth
Thank you for your intelligence
Thank you for your humor
Thank you for your strength
Thank you for your caring ways
Thank you for your daily texts
During virus-isolation
I love your brown hair and bright eyes
I love your exuberance
I love your devotion to friends
Adaline and Hayden -
I love your love of your dogs
I love your cupcakes
I love your heart and mind
I love you
Now and forever
Onward!

POEM #201287

White wall, Spanish, textured,
scarlet cushion,
Gregorian chants from Hungary,
a whistle
(in the background a commercial)
my black pen moving
left - to - right
a bubble-uble—ing
goldfish swim in random patterns,
I clear my throat
and think
and what of this
and what is this
that is or is it
or is it not an it at all
or not at all
or all or nothing

my eyes blink, tight, tired, dry,
from crying,
from happiness

Gracias a Dios,
last night,
Bach's B Minor Mass,
this morning's mass,
Armenian Orthodox and
painting my door ivory,
a ham sandwich,
sitting on our balcony

with my wife and hot tea
darkness comes

Thanks be to God
God be thanked
Be God and thankful
Full of God and being
Be full and still
Still

White wall, Spanish, textured,
scarlet cushion,
Gregorian chants (from Hungary)

Here in Caracas
in our monastery

Thanks to the Most High
Glory be to Thee on High
All thanks and glory be Thine
All mine and
Mind is All in All

Listen to the song
the singing rises, falls and rises again,
brooding, sitting, setting
and back and forth,
the Middle Ages to Robocop
the Buddha almost smiles,
the mirror, reflections of reality
the path to the forest shrine, and
The books, papered, colored,
In disorderly rows

to be read and
what was said, oh
my head,
to get ahead,
go ahead,
little shepherd
seeking the child
Jesus
O barefoot kid yourself
who grew up to bare
yourself before God as
heir and before humanity as
sibling
Thank you
O Lamb of God who taketh
away the illusions of this world
and who taketh us to
the mysteries of the Other World
in the midst of this world
Glory be to Thee

Lightness, rising and falling and
rising again
and is dinner ready
and will I be ready
already willing
already being
and what of you?

BALANCE. HOW MAINTAIN IT?

Balance. How maintain it?
The still point. How be it?
Everything in motion except
My soul.
Dis-identify with the first
Four bodies
Identify with bliss, consciousness,
The Implicate, the Other World,
God, Mystery.
Be the Universal, the Ocean,
Let the Particular do its dance
As the wave, rising, splashing,
Falling
The Ultimate Mystery, the
Ultimate Power, the
Ultimate Reality
Love

DIALOGUE AND DANCING

The most dangerous belief is that
My belief is the only true belief and that
Other beliefs must be eradicated

The vilest interest is found in
My interest as the only worthy interest with
Other interests to be ignored

The most beautiful belief is that
My belief is very good and that
Other's beliefs should also be respected

The most wonderful interest is that
My interest is very important and that
Other interests should also be honored

Neither absolutism nor relativism
But right down the middle
A deepening dialogue
Among beliefs
A dynamic dance
Among interests

Let the dialogue begin!
Let the dance begin!

LETTING GO

I let go of my two grandmothers,
I let go of my father,
I let go of my wife,
I have let go of so much,
But there is so much more
To let go of

I let go of Oklahoma,
I let go of Chicago,
I let go of Malaysia,
I let go of Korea,
I let go of Jamaica,
I let go of Venezuela,
I let go of Manhattan,
I let go of Larchmont,
I let go of Peekskill,
Yet there is so much more
To let go of

I let go of my infancy,
I let go of my boyhood,
I let go of my young adulthood,
I let go of the Ecumenical Institute,
I let go of the Institute of Cultural Affairs,
I let go of the Order Ecumenical
I let go of my marriage,
I let go of my two sons,
Yet there is so much more
To let go of

I will let go of my mother,
I will let go of the United Nations,
I will let go of Garrison,
I will let go of the Hudson Valley,
I will let go of my life

Yet in letting go we do not lose
That which we once had
But have it still for eternity
Ever changing
Ever continuous
Ever present

I let go

PAY ATTENTION!

Pay attention!
This is it!
No other moment!
No other life!
Give thanks for blessings!
Pay attention!
Don't miss it!
This is it!

AT THE STILL POINT

Spinning, Rotating
Swinging, Encircling
Spiraling, Turning
Sweeping, Orbiting

All is circular
All is mandala
All is in motion
All is perfect
At the still point

Why are we out of sorts?
Why do we suffer?
Why do we cause suffering?

O, but the view!
There is only the Dance!
The ecstasy to be.

May everyone have space
To be and to dance.

IT IS POSSIBLE

It is possible, yes it is
Do not despair. Do not drown
   in sorrow and fear, in anger and pride.
Remember the beauty of a happy baby,
A white rose, a stunning sunset, the night sky
Filled with trillions of stars
Be grateful for the gift of life

Wake up, wake up!
This is it. We *can* change history.
Our decisions and actions
   created this world.
We can *invent* a different world.
Yes, you and I can do it

Let the trans-formation begin with me.
I plunge into myself, my own body,
   emotions and mind.
I face my demons and fears
I face my anger and hatred
My own pride and greed
And I let it go
I let it go and in exchange I receive
A new world

A world of trust and joy,
A world of happiness and wisdom,
A world of compassion and kindness
A world of acceptance and gratitude

With the smell and taste of freshness,
Here and now
Yes!
Let's do it now!

In this new world
empty of a separate self
full of all that is not I
manifesting compassion
reaching out
forgiving my enemies
relieving suffering
wherever it is found
Yes, it is possible
Let's do it now!

JUST BE

Just be
Just not be
Just let go of both
For there is only the
One
And even that one
Does not exist

GREETINGS

Greetings, dear John, Thea, David, Pat, Larry,
Peggy, Jan, Richard,
and other friends of the Way!
A voice came out of the past
But actually the present
No, it was the future calling
No again,
It was Mary from the Other World saying
Rob, you should go to the retreat, dear.
Yes, dear, you are right
I am going-coming
With my sorrow-joy
With my body-mind
I am going-coming
To study the self
Knowing that there is no self
Therefore, we can call it the self
I am going-coming
To save all sentient beings
Knowing that there are no sentient beings
Therefore, we can say that there are sentient beings
I go to the Eternal Present
I go to the Fullness of Mind
Simply to sit
Simply to be
With my friends
In Mystery
May we each realize peace, happiness, wisdom
and compassion!

IS THE FOG SAD?

i.
Is the fog sad?
Is the dead dog in the river sad?
This body of water is sad
The Hudson is not sad

ii.
The train takes me once again
To where I don't want to go
To where I know not
Yet, I ride

iii.
Here, fog and rain
Gray and brown landscape
There, sun and sea
Purple azaleas and white sand

iv.
Tired and confused
Just want to rest
To be clear
To be happy

v.
Spring is coming
Will it bring life or death

Or both?
Yes, and we must accept

vi.
gold on silver, silver on gold
try as we may
flesh can never become me
yet, still we must try

vii.
Today the sun is shining
But inside is dark
I don't know why
Yet, I live it

viii.
Is there something that
Doesn't let me be happy
That stops me
When I am?

ix.
Too many demands
Everyone wants a part of me
But is there enough
To go around?

x.
Blink, breathe
Be grateful

For being
Alive

xi.
White velvet
Buddha's birthday

I VOW TO BE HAPPY

I vow to be happy
I vow to be true
I vow to be kind
I vow to be myself
I vow to serve all
I vow to give my best
I vow to be grateful
I vow to be generous
I vow to be patient
I vow to remember
 my vows when I forget
 which surely I will.

Yes, I have been angry
I have been angry at death
I have been angry at criticism
I have been angry at mistrust
I have been angry at woundedness
I have been angry at old age
I have been angry at sickness
I have been angry at impotence
I have been angry at the wealthy
I have been angry at the political elites
I have been angry about poverty
I have been angry about climate chaos
I have been angry about police brutality
I have been angry about injustices of all kinds

I love the sun and sunshine

I love blue skies and white clouds
I love warm, clean air
I love spiral galaxies
I love French horns
I love the Buddha way
I love my children
I love my grandchildren
I love flowers of all kinds but especially sunflowers
I love blueberries
I love blogging
I love teaching
I love facilitating
I love journaling
I love meditating
I love the color yellow
I love New York City
I love making others happy
I love empowering others
I love helping others reflect
I love reflecting

SUNSHINE FLOODING
LANDSCAPE AND EYESCAPE

Sunshine flooding landscape and eyescape
Green everywhere, trees, grass, stems, ivy
Dancing with my beloved upon waking
A quiet homespace
Water running, shadows on the floor
Hot shower, typing fingers moving
Mind open, hearing, seeing
Pictures of family, Earth, bodhisattvas
Old wood, bamboo, wicker, ceramics
Icons everywhere, cushion, altar
Decades remembered, a present moment
Full of feelings, thoughts, anticipations
Tapas lunch with my beloved
Pizza dinner and ice cream with grandkids
Tomorrow's party in our home filled with family
What is this life? For me, for others?How create a
world that works for everyone?

A 75TH BIRTHDAY POEM

Seven and one half decades
Long or short? A lot or a little?
For a star, very short,
For a lizard, very long,
For a human, fairly long,
So much love received
And much given
So much gratitude
Some grief, more joy
A life lived
And here with you
Dear family and friends
I am aware that time
Is quickly passing
Just yesterday Catherine,
Phoenix, and Mariela
Were babies,
Now look at them!
In fact we were all
Babies and now look
At us!
And soon enough our
Time will end
And we will be sad
But keep on living and
Loving
Let's give it our all.
What is that for you?
For me it is writing books,
Being a climate/justice activist,

Nurturing my family
Caring for my health in
Body and mind
That may be enough
And how long do we have?
1 second? 1 year?
Ten years? 100 years?
It is enough to live and
To love
Let's do it

ACKNOWLEDGMENTS

Gratitude to Emily Dickinson, Walt Whitman, e. e. cummings. T. S. Eliot, Carl Sandburg, Robert Frost, D. H. Lawrence, Nikos Kazantzakis, Rumi, and Rilke, for their poems which have inspired me over the years.

Gratitude to Laura J. Bauer, Dr. Nikhil Chandavarkar, Peggy Rubin, Dr. Larry Ward, and Dr. Qinghong Wei, for their pre-publication reviews and endorsements.

Gratitude to my English teachers in grad school, university and high school for helping awaken my love for the English language, especially the writings of the English and American poets of the 20th century.

Gratitude to Dr. Jean Houston and Peggy Rubin for calling forth my creativity in thought, language, and dance, in many years of Mystery School.

Gratitude to my wife, Bonnie Myotai Treace, for her love, advice, and support for this publication.

Gratitude to my late wife, Mary Elizabeth Avery Work, for sharing her poetry, art, and life with me.

NOTES

Apologia Poetica: 1984, Kingston, Jamaica; a poem is . .

Collection One:
Poems Celebrating Earth and Humanity
Starlight Burns: 2003, Garrison, New York; sunshine from our nearest star
Earthrise Alive: 1984, Kingston, Jamaica; the Overview effect (seeing the Earth from space is transformative)
The Wonder of Being a Speck: 2005, Garrison
Every Day Is Earth Day: 2014, Cold Spring, New York; first published in *A Compassionate Civilization,* 2017, (ACC)
Earthling Vows: 2013, Cold Spring; first published in ACC
In Celebration of Mt. Avila: 1988, Caracas, Venezuela
Only This: 2003, Garrison
Earth Had a Dream: 1990, Caracas; first published in ACC
Ducks Swimming in a Row: 2003, Garrison
A Gift Given: 1984, Kingston; first published in *Serving People & Planet,* 2020 (SPP)
Hudson River Moments: 2003, Garrison; celebrating the

historic river flowing both ways, inland to the Atlantic; alongside of which I commuted by train for many years
Spinning, Whirling, Earth, and Air: 2003, Garrison
The Divine Comedy: No Joke: 2014, Cold Spring; first published in ACC; remembering Dante
We Are a Human Being First: 2014, Cold Spring; first published in ACC; one species, cosmic Earthlings
For W.I.T.: 1988, Caracas; a tribute to philosopher William Irwin Thompson
The Still Point at the Center: 2003, Garrison
For My Colleagues of the Way: 1988, Caracas
Domingo: 1988, Caracas (Sunday in Spanish)
Poem #201287.2: 1987, Caracas
GNIEB: 1988, Caracas; title is BEING backwards
The Search Is Ended: 1988, Caracas
For Now: 1988, Caracas
Poem #211287: 1987, Caracas
The Precious Gifts: 2003, Garrison
The Word: This Is It!: 2014, Cold Spring; first published in ACC
And They Set Forth: 1990, New York City; written to celebrate the Whole System Think Tank Meeting with Jean Houston, PhD, in Bocono, Venezuela
Appreciating Both Process and Results: 2000, New York, City; for an Appreciative Inquiry UN workshop
A Mythic Journey: 1993, Peekskill, NY; written for an event at the Wainwright House in Rye, NY, led by Jean Houston, PhD
Sentiments on a Blue and Gold Cub Scout: 1965, Stillwater,

OK; first published in Oklahoma State University's journal "Soliloquy"; one of author's five first published poems (1963-65)

Peace, Yes!: 2003, Garrison; peace march in NYC

War Is Terrorism: 2003, Garrison; first published in ACC

Autumn View: 2003, Garrison

I Am Sick, but . . . : 2003, Garrison

Collection Two:
Poems Commemorating Family and Self

Grand Mother Duncan: 1984, Kingston, Jamaica; she lived in Durant, Oklahoma

Three-fold Kindness Prayer: 2003, Garrison

Mary: 1984, Kingston; author's wife

A Family Transparency: 1974, Seoul, Republic of Korea, on the adoption of the author's first son Benjamin

Benjamin: 1984, Kingston

Christopher: 1984, Kingston; author's second son

Where Are You?: 2003, Garrison; after the death of author's wife from cancer

Decide and Choose: 2003, Garrison

A Lady with a Red Rose: 2003, Garrison

I Am Not Afraid: 2003, Garrison

Hillside Cottage: 2003, Garrison; our home

Life Is for the Living: 2003, Garrison

Live and Die Fully: 2003, Garrison

Going to Manhattan Once Again: 2003, Garrison

Mary, I Love You Still: 2003, Garrison

My Wife, My Life: 2003, Garrison

Prayer: 2003, Garrison
Everything That Comes To Be: 2003, Garrison
They Set Out: 2004, Garrison; written for Christopher and Jennifer on their trip westward
The Vision Quest: 2004, Garrison; written for Christopher and Jennifer
Dancing on Water: 2006, Garrison; written for Bonnie; and the next eight poems
Clouds White: 2006, Garrison
Heart of Love: 2006, Garrison
Two Lovers: 2006, Garrison
Ten Kisses: 2006, Garrison
Engagement Poem: 2006, Garrison
Lightest of Blue: 2006, Garrison
Wave Swirls Clouds Light: 2007, Delphi, Greece; written on boat trip with Bonnie from Ithaca to Delphi
Honeymoon: 2007, Haliburton, Canada
A Tribute to Mothers: 2014, Cold Spring; first published in ACC
My Christmas Eve Baby: 2018, Swannanoa, North Carolina; written for Christopher
Thanksgiving 2019: 2019, Swannanoa; for family in North Carolina
WOW, POW!: 2020, Swannanoa; for grandson Phoenix
Celebrating You: 2020, Swannanoa; for granddaughter Mariela
Poem #201287.3: 1987, Caracas
Balance, How Maintain It?: 2003, Garrison
Dialogue and Dancing: 2003, Garrison
Letting Go: 2003, Garrison

Pay Attention!: 2003, Garrison
At the Still Point: 2003, Garrison
It Is Possible: 2003, Garrison
Just Be: 2003, Garrison
Greetings: 2004, Garrison; going to a retreat in Oklahoma
   led by Drs. Larry and Peggy Ward
Is the Fog Sad?: 2006, Garrison
I Vow To Be Happy: 2015, Cold Spring
Sunshine Flooding Landscape and Eyescape: 2015,
   Swannanoa; on author's birthday
A 75th Birthday Poem: 2019, Swannanoa

ABOUT THE AUTHOR

M oorman Robertson Work Jr. is a nonfiction author and ecosystem/justice activist. Robertson has published two previous books, an autobiography, *Serving People & Planet: In Mystery, Love, and Gratitude,* and a manifesto/handbook, *A Compassionate Civilization: The Urgency of Sustainable Development and Mindful Activism,* and contributed to eleven others. He and his wife live in Swannanoa, North Carolina, close to family, friends, and the Great Smoky Mountains. Having worked in over fifty countries for over fifty years, he was UNDP deputy-director of the democratic governance division and principal policy adviser for decentralized governance, NYU Wagner Graduate School of Public Service adjunct professor of innovative leadership for sustainable development, and Institute of Cultural Affairs (ICA) executive-director in four countries, conducting community, organizational, and leadership initiatives.

He may be contacted at robertsonwork100@gmail. com. His blogsite is at: https://compassionateciviliza-tion.blogspot.com/